# Understanding and Thriving with Your ADHD Boyfriend

## Navigating Life with a Partner with ADHD

### Rachel J. Oles

# Table of Contents

# <u>INTRODUCTION</u>

Dear Reader,

Welcome to "When Your Boyfriend Has ADHD." As the author of this book, I am delighted to begin this journey with you, examining the complexity, challenges, and joys of being in a relationship with a partner who has Attention Deficit Hyperactivity Disorder (ADHD).

Through these pages, I wish to provide you with insights, understanding, and practical techniques to traverse this particular path with compassion, patience, and love.

Writing this book derives from my personal experience and enthusiasm for fostering healthy and rewarding relationships. Having been in a relationship with a partner who has ADHD, I have encountered both the hardships and successes that come with loving someone with this illness.

Throughout my journey, I have grown to appreciate that ADHD is not a handicap but rather a unique feature of the person I love.

In the beginning, I, too, encountered worries and questions about how ADHD would affect our relationship. I questioned how we could handle the obstacles that developed due to ADHD symptoms such as impulsivity, forgetfulness, and difficulty with time management.

However, when I looked deeper into understanding ADHD and its effects on relationships, I discovered that empathy and open communication were the keys to developing a firm foundation for our love.

In publishing this book, my purpose is to offer you a supportive guide that addresses the numerous parts of being in a relationship with a spouse who has ADHD. I will not only present the science behind ADHD but also go into the emotional and practical factors that frequently go hand in hand with this illness.

Together, we will examine communication tactics, ways to manage emotions, and strategies to create closeness and connection.

This book is not a one-size-fits-all answer, but rather a toolkit filled with knowledge and techniques that you may customize to your situation.

Whether you are in a long-term relationship or just beginning to navigate the obstacles of ADHD, my aim is that you will find help, reassurance, and inspiration within these pages.

Throughout this journey, I encourage you to remember that love knows no limits, and relationships grow when fostered with understanding, patience, and kindness.

I ask you to embrace the qualities and beauty that come with loving someone with ADHD and to go on a path of growth and connection together. In the chapters that follow, we will delve into the intricacies of ADHD and its impact on relationships.

Thank you for entrusting me with your journey, and I hope that "When Your Boyfriend Has ADHD" will serve as a guiding light on the path to developing a loving, caring, and happy relationship with your partner.

With compassion and understanding,

Rachel J. Oles.

# Chapter 1

## <u>UNDERSTANDING ADHD</u>

Attention Deficit Hyperactivity Disorder (ADHD) is divided into three basic groups, each with its unique set of symptoms and characteristics. These classifications are based on the key symptoms an individual exhibits, and the presentation of ADHD might vary across different age groups. Let's study the three kinds of ADHD in detail:

**1. Predominantly Inattentive Presentation (ADHD-I):**
Predominantly Inattentive Presentation, commonly known as ADHD-I, is characterized by severe difficulty with attention and focus while displaying limited hyperactive or impulsive behaviors.

Individuals with ADHD-I may have trouble sustaining concentration on tasks, resulting in challenges with organization, time management, and finishing chores. Common symptoms of ADHD-I include:

- Difficulty paying attention to details and making careless blunders in schoolwork, job, or other activities.

- Inability to maintain concentrated on duties, discussions, or hobbies, even when they are engaging or necessary.

- Struggling to listen attentively and follow through on instructions or directions.

- Frequently losing objects needed for everyday activities, such as keys, books, or cell phones.

- Being forgetful in regular chores, such as finishing housework or maintaining appointments.

**2. Predominantly Hyperactive-Impulsive Presentation (ADHD-HI):**

Predominantly Hyperactive-Impulsive Presentation, commonly known as ADHD-HI, is characterized by mainly hyperactive and impulsive behaviors, with moderate inattention.

Individuals with ADHD-HI may appear restless, and fidgety, and may have trouble keeping sat or staying immobile when it is expected. Common symptoms of ADHD-HI include:

- Constantly fidgeting with hands or feet or squirming when seated.

- Difficulty keeping sat in contexts when staying seated is expected, including classes or meetings.

- Feeling restless and being "on the go" as though powered by a motor.

- Talking excessively or blurting forth replies before inquiry are concluded.

- Interrupting or interfering with others' chats, games, or pastimes.

**3. Combined Presentation (ADHD-C):**
Combined Presentation, usually known as ADHD-C, is the most frequent type of ADHD. It involves a combination of both inattentive and hyperactive-impulsive tendencies.

Individuals with ADHD-C may exhibit a broad range of symptoms, including those from both the mostly inattentive and predominantly hyperactive-impulsive varieties. Common symptoms of ADHD-C include:

- Difficulty paying attention and remaining focused on chores or talks.

- Restlessness and trouble staying still in situations that require calm and focus.

- Impulsive conduct, such as acting without thinking through the ramifications or interrupting others.

It is crucial to note that ADHD is a complex and multifaceted disorder, and its symptoms can emerge differently across different age groups.

For instance, hyperactive tendencies may be more noticeable in younger children, while inattention may become more apparent as individuals grow older. Additionally, those with ADHD may confront special challenges in job, relationships, and time management.

The diagnosis of ADHD demands a complete evaluation by a trained healthcare specialist, taking into account the individual's history, symptoms, and the impact of these symptoms on their everyday functioning. Early diagnosis and proper support can help individuals with ADHD manage their symptoms efficiently and enjoy fulfilling lives.

A combination of behavioral therapy, educational aid, and, in some instances, medication can be crucial components of a comprehensive treatment plan adapted to each person's particular needs.

## SYMPTOMS OF ADHD IN ADULTS

ADHD, generally associated with youngsters, is a neurological disorder that can persist into adulthood. However, the symptoms of ADHD in adults can manifest differently compared to adolescents.

Adult ADHD is often characterized by trouble in executive functioning, emotional regulation, and relationships. It is crucial to remember that not all individuals with ADHD present the same symptoms, and the severity of these symptoms can vary from person to person. Here is a detailed look at the indications of ADHD in adults:

## 1. Inattention:

- Difficulty paying attention to details and making careless blunders in employment, school, or daily activities.

- Struggling to keep focus during work or conversations, leading to poor follow-through on tasks.

- Frequently losing objects needed for routine chores, such as keys, wallets, or important documents.

- Easily distracted by external stimuli or internal thoughts, making it harder to concentrate on critical activities.

**2. Impulsivity:**
- Acting or speaking without thinking through the consequences, leading to frequent social or interpersonal difficulties.

- Difficulty waiting for one's turn in situations that require patience, such as standing in lines or waiting for others to complete speaking.

- Impulsive decision-making, leading to rapid changes in plans or partaking in harmful behaviors without analyzing possible implications.

**3. Hyperactivity (often internal):**
- Feeling restless or having a sensation of inner restlessness, which may not be as obvious in overt bodily movements.

- Experiencing racing thoughts or having trouble quieting the mind when trying to relax or go to sleep.

- Feeling an internal sense of agitation or being "on the go" mentally, even when physically still.

## 4. Executive Functioning Challenges:
- Struggling with time management and organization, resulting to missed deadlines and difficulty in managing everyday chores.

- Having trouble prioritizing things and finishing them in an effective and organized manner.

- Difficulty with planning and problem-solving, which may appear in work-related duties or personal decision-making.

## 5. Emotional Dysregulation:
- Experiencing excessive emotional reactions to situations, leading to mood swings or emotional outbursts.

- Difficulty managing annoyance or anger, leading to impulsive or reactive behaviors.

- Feeling overwhelmed by stress or criticism, leading to heightened emotional responses.

**6. Relationship Difficulties:**
- Struggling with maintaining long-term relationships owing to challenges in communication, attentiveness, and emotional regulation.

- Experiencing difficulties in empathizing with others' opinions or interpreting social cues during encounters.

- Difficulty planning and managing family, professional, or social commitments, leading to strained relationships.

**7. Procrastination and Avoidance:**

- Tending to postpone or delay things that need continual mental effort or focus.

- Avoiding jobs that are monotonous or unstimulating, resulting in difficulty in finishing them.

**8. Impaired Memory:**
- Forgetting appointments, commitments, or major occasions regularly.

- Having trouble retaining facts or information from recent discussions or activities.

It is important to understand that the symptoms of adult ADHD can dramatically impede daily life, including job, education, relationships, and overall well-being.

However, it is also crucial to understand that adults with ADHD can utilize unique abilities such as creativity, adaptability, and out-of-the-box thinking.

For a comprehensive diagnosis of adult ADHD, a thorough evaluation by a skilled healthcare practitioner is recommended. Additionally, other medical or psychological disorders must be ruled out before receiving a solid diagnosis of ADHD.

Managing adult ADHD frequently needs a variety of treatments, such as cognitive-behavioral therapy, medication, lifestyle adjustments, and support systems. Early recognition and intervention can drastically enhance the quality of life for those with ADHD, helping them negotiate their barriers and leverage their strengths for personal growth and achievement.

# Chapter 2

## DEBUNKING COMMON MISCONCEPTIONS

ADHD in adults is a phenomenon that is often misunderstood, leading to several misconceptions regarding its prevalence, symptoms, and impact on everyday life.

Addressing these beliefs is crucial for having a correct knowledge and delivering help to adults with ADHD. Let's address some widespread myths concerning ADHD in adults and provide clarification on the subject:

**1. Misconception: ADHD only affects children.**
- **Truth:** ADHD is a lifelong neurodevelopmental condition that can persist into adulthood. While symptoms may fluctuate over time, many folks

continue to face challenges related to ADHD throughout their adult lives.

## 2. Misconception: ADHD is a result of poor parenting or a lack of discipline.

**Truth:** ADHD is a neurological condition with a strong genetic component. It is not caused by parenting practices or discipline. Environmental factors may alter the expression of ADHD symptoms, but they do not cause the disorder.

## 3. Misconception: Adults with ADHD are just unorganized or forgetful.

**Truth:** While disorganization and forgetfulness are prevalent symptoms in adults with ADHD, the disorder encompasses more severe impairments with executive functioning, focus, impulse control, and emotional regulation.

**4. Misconception: Adults with ADHD are less intellectual or capable.**

- **<u>Truth:</u>** ADHD does not impair IQ, and many adults with ADHD are highly intelligent and gifted. However, the condition could impair executive functioning, resulting in difficulty in managing activities and duties successfully.

**5. Misconception: Adults with ADHD can outgrow or overcome the disorder.**

**<u>Truth:</u>** While some individuals may gain coping skills to manage their symptoms effectively, ADHD remains a neurological condition that continues throughout life. Managing symptoms often takes continual guidance and approaches.

**6. Misconception: ADHD medicines are just for youngsters and can be overused by adults.**

- **<u>Truth:</u>** ADHD medicines can be suggested for adults to assist manage symptoms and boost daily functioning. When prescribed and overseen by a skilled healthcare provider, these medicines can be safe and effective for people with ADHD.

## 7. Misconception: Adults with ADHD are merely lazy or uninspired.

- **Truth:** Adults with ADHD may struggle with motivation due to issues with executive functioning. They may find it difficult to commence work, prioritize, or hold concentration, which may be perceived as lazy.

## 8. Misconception: ADHD is not a serious condition.

- **Truth:** ADHD can substantially impede an adult's daily life, employment, education, and relationships. The problems related with the sickness might generate emotional agony and harm general well-being.

**9. Misconception: Adults with ADHD are hyperactive and frequently fidgety.**

- <u>**Truth:**</u> While hyperactivity is one indication of ADHD, it may manifest differently in adults. Some folks with ADHD may have more internal restlessness rather than overt physical hyperactivity.

**10. Misconception: Adults with ADHD can control their symptoms if they try harder.**

<u>**Truth:**</u> ADHD is not a matter of willpower or effort. It is a neurological disorder that requires understanding, support, and effective strategies to control symptoms.

**11. Misconception: ADHD exclusively affects men.**

- <u>**Truth:**</u> ADHD is not gender-specific and can affect both men and women. However, it may be underdiagnosed in women due to differences in symptom presentation and societal expectations.

**12. Misconception: Adults with ADHD are always unorganized and unruly.**

- **<u>Truth:</u>** While disorganization can be an issue for some individuals with ADHD, others may find coping mechanisms that help them preserve structure and order in their lives.

**13. Misconception: Adults with ADHD are always talkative and hyperactive.**
**<u>Truth:</u>** ADHD symptoms could develop differently in adults. While some may experience hyperactivity and impulsivity, others may primarily deal with inattention, making them appear reserved or quiet.

**14. Misconception: Adults with ADHD are unreliable and cannot be counted on.**
- **<u>Truth:</u>** ADHD can make it difficult to regularly satisfy expectations, but it does not mean that adults with ADHD are inherently unreliable. With sufficient guidance and

methods, people may complete their commitments efficiently.

## 15. Misconception: Adults with ADHD are not successful in their careers.

- **Truth:** Many adults with ADHD have successful jobs in many sectors. Their resourcefulness, perseverance, and aptitude to think beyond the box might be assets in certain vocations.

## 16. Misconception: ADHD is a minor condition that does not require attention or support.

- **Truth:** ADHD can drastically damage various elements of an adult's life, including relationships, education, and profession. Proper diagnosis and assistance are crucial for reducing symptoms and enhancing quality of life.

**17. Misconception: Adults with ADHD are lazy or lack initiative.**

- **Truth:** ADHD-related concerns, such as trouble with organization and time management, may lead to productivity issues. However, persons with ADHD can be enormously motivated and ambitious in things that attract their interest and love.

**18. Misconception: Medication is the only treatment for ADHD.**

**Truth:** While medication can be an effective treatment for managing ADHD symptoms, other measures, such as therapy, coaching, and lifestyle adjustments, can also play a major role in managing the disorder.

**19. Misconception: ADHD is caused by too much screen time or modern technology.**

- **Truth:** ADHD has a neurological foundation and is not caused by technology use. While excessive screen time may exacerbate inattention, it is not the underlying cause of ADHD.

**20. Misconception: Adults with ADHD cannot have good relationships or be excellent parents.**
- **Truth:** With awareness, understanding, and support, adults with ADHD may maintain strong and happy relationships and succeed as parents. Open communication and reciprocal empathy are key components in creating healthy marriages and parental interactions.

Addressing these beliefs is crucial to establish a more empathetic and supportive culture for individuals with ADHD. Increased awareness and understanding can lead to less stigma, increased access to resources, and enhanced possibilities for personal and professional growth.

Emphasizing individual strengths, encouraging self-advocacy, and understanding the diverse experiences of individuals with ADHD can lead to a more inclusive and accepting atmosphere for everyone.

# Chapter 3

## <u>ADHD AND RELATIONSHIPS</u>

ADHD can bring specific hurdles to a love connection, influencing both partners in various ways.

These difficulties stem from the basic symptoms of ADHD, such as inattention, impulsivity, hyperactivity (often internal), and executive functioning deficiencies. Let's analyze these challenges in greater detail:

**1. Communication Difficulties:**
- Individuals with ADHD may have problems with active listening and may appear distracted during talks.

- Inattentiveness can lead to misinterpretation and misconceptions, reducing the quality of communication in the relationship.

- Impulsivity could result in speaking things without thinking through the ramifications, resulting in damaged feelings or disagreements.

## 2. Time Management and Organization:

- Difficulties with time management could lead to tardiness, missed appointments, or changes in plans, generating discontent or disappointment in the partner.

- Challenges in arranging might result in cluttered living surroundings and a lack of regularity, hurting both partners' daily routines.

## 3. Emotional Regulation:

- Emotional dysregulation can generate severe mood swings or emotional outbursts, leading to stress and conflict within the couple.

- The spouse may feel overwhelmed by their loved one's emotional responses and struggle to offer support or understanding.

## 4. Impulsivity and Risky Behaviors:
- Impulsivity can lead to quick judgments, particularly financial decisions, without comprehending the repercussions.

- Risk-taking behaviors may raise concern for the spouse, especially if it jeopardizes the couple's well-being or safety.

## 5. Forgetfulness and Inattention to Details:
- Forgetfulness can lead to disregarding critical relationship obligations or special occasions, making the partner feel unimportant or worthless.

- Inattention to details may result in forgetting the partner's needs or desires, leading to sentiments of being neglected or unappreciated.

## 6. Uneven Distribution of Responsibilities:

- The partner without ADHD may find themselves taking on more responsibility in the relationship, leading to feelings of imbalance or burnout.

- This can generate tension and frustration if the non-ADHD spouse perceives their efforts as unreciprocated.

## 7. Difficulty with Follow-Through:

- The partner with ADHD may struggle to follow through on pledges or obligations, leading to a loss of confidence and disappointment.

- This could produce misunderstanding and unhappiness inside the partnership.

## 8. Time Together vs. Alone Time:

- The spouse with ADHD may need isolation or downtime to recharge, which could differ from their partner's expectations or ambitions for meaningful time together.

- The non-ADHD partner may mistake this desire for separation, leading to feelings of rejection or estrangement.

**9. Stress & Overwhelm:**
- The hurdles linked with ADHD, like performing everyday activities and responsibilities, can generate tension and overload for both couples.

- Stress can strain the relationship and harm emotional closeness and intimacy.

**10. Intimacy and Emotional Connection:**
- The fluctuations in emotional control and attention may harm the emotional intimacy and connection between spouses.

- Both partners may struggle to feel emotionally connected or understood, leading to feelings of estrangement.

Continuing to manage the specific challenges that ADHD can bring to a loving relationship, both parties need to adopt a kind and patient approach. Here are some other elements to consider:

## 11. Personal Growth and Self-Empowerment:

- The partner with ADHD may endure unhappiness or self-doubt owing to the issues they confront daily.

- Encouraging personal growth and self-empowerment might be vital in strengthening their confidence and resilience.

- Recognizing and appreciating their successes, no matter how modest, may foster a good and supportive workplace.

Each relationship is unique, and no union is without its problems. The purpose is to handle the difficulties with compassion, resilience, and a determination to grow together.

Through open communication, empathy, and a shared commitment to assist each other, couples can build a strong and loving bond that exceeds the problems provided by ADHD. Embracing the journey as a team and cherishing the moments of joy and connection can make the relationship not just endure but also thrive.

# Chapter 4

## <u>ADVANTAGES OF ADHD</u>

Having a spouse with ADHD can offer unique and beneficial aspects to a relationship, strengthening it in ways that may not be as apparent in marriages without ADHD.

While ADHD might bring hurdles, it also comes with intrinsic characteristics that can be appreciated and valued. Here are some favorable benefits of having a partner with ADHD:

**1. Creativity:** Individuals with ADHD generally display a remarkable level of creativity. Their capacity to think outside the box, detect connections others might overlook, and develop innovative ideas can fire the collaboration with passion and fresh insights.

**2. Spontaneity:** ADHD can bring a sense of spontaneity and adventure to the connection. The partner's readiness to welcome the unexpected and pursue new experiences can offer a feeling of excitement and enjoyment to the daily routine.

**3. Zest:** People with ADHD could display a contagious zest for life. Their energy and excitement for new activities or interests can inspire their spouse to explore and live life to the fullest.

**4. Energy:** ADHD can be accompanied by a surplus of energy, which can be infectious and energizing for the relationship. Their passion can inject a sense of life and motivation into joint actions.

**5. Compassion and Empathy:** Having weathered their own issues related with ADHD, those with the disorder usually develop a heightened feeling of compassion and empathy. This information can build a helpful and caring environment in the partnership.

**6. Flexibility:** ADHD can develop flexibility and adaption in the spouse. They may be more open to adjusting plans or trying new techniques, which can make the relationship more dynamic and attentive to each partner's needs.

**7. Humor:** Many individuals with ADHD display a terrific sense of humor. Their capacity to uncover comedy in ordinary events can help reduce stress and offer delight to the partnership.

**8. Tenacity:** Managing the challenges of ADHD demands tenacity and perseverance. Individuals with ADHD frequently have excellent coping qualities that could help the connection through challenging periods.

**9. Open-Mindedness:** The partner's ability to observe things from numerous aspects can lead to open-mindedness and an appreciation for diverse opinions in the relationship.

**10. Supportive of distinctiveness:** People with ADHD typically embrace their originality and unique quirks. This acceptance can extend to their marriage, creating an environment where both individuals feel encouraged to be their actual selves.

**11. Passion for Interests:** When someone with ADHD is passionate about anything, they can become totally immersed in it. This degree of attention can be contagious and lead to shared pursuits and hobbies inside the partnership.

**12. Spreading Joy:** The spontaneous and lively nature of the spouse with ADHD can bring joy and laughter to the partnership.

Their playfulness can lift the emotions of their spouse and infuse the partnership with positivity.

**13. Hyperfocus:** While ADHD could involve difficulties with sustained attention, it can also lead to hyperfocus on tasks or hobbies that captivate the partner's attention. This acute focus can result in excellent productivity and dedication to job or interests.

**14. Intuition and Emotional Sensitivity:** People with ADHD can be extraordinarily intuitive and emotionally sensitive. They may have a great ability to perceive their partner's feelings and wishes, producing a profound emotional connection in the relationship.

**15. Adventurous Spirit:** The spouse with ADHD may appreciate adventure and novelty, making them open to attempting new things and exploring the world together. This risky approach can produce enduring experiences and deepen the bond between partners.

**16. Empowerment of Others:** Individuals with ADHD may display a desire to empower and uplift those around them. They generally celebrate their partner's accomplishments and offer support during bad times, fostering personal growth and well-being.

**17. Thinking on Their Feet:** The partner's capacity to think quickly and adapt can be an asset in problem-solving and handling unforeseen scenarios. This nimbleness can contribute to good communication and settlement of difficulties.

**18. Uncommon Solutions:** With their creative thinking, folks with ADHD may come up with innovative and uncommon solutions to situations. This resourcefulness can lead to out-of-the-box approaches that enrich the connection.

**19. Emotional Intensity:** The spouse with ADHD may experience emotions powerfully, leading to times of tremendous joy and passion. This emotional depth can develop essential and personal relationships within the partnership.

**20. True and Authentic:** People with ADHD often display a true and authentic nature, without pretense or artifice. This transparency can build trust and a strong sense of connection between partners.

**21. Empathy and Sensitivity to Others' Struggles:** Having endured their own adversities, individuals with ADHD can be especially empathetic and tolerant toward others' struggles. This empathy can make them nice and helpful companions.

**22. Ability to Multitask:** While multitasking can be challenging for some persons, those with ADHD may excel in handling several tasks simultaneously, making them adept in managing various obligations in the relationship.

**23. Energetic and Playful Parenting:** The partner's energetic disposition can extend to parenting, making them engaging and fun-loving parents. This playfulness can improve the parent-child bond and generate a joyful family climate.

**24. Passionate in Relationships:** People with ADHD may demonstrate passion and intensity in romantic relationships, leading to deep attachments and a sensation of being truly cherished.

**25. Non-Judgmental Attitude:** Individuals with ADHD usually grasp the significance of judgment and may create a non-judgmental attitude toward their spouse and others. This acceptance can generate a nurturing and supportive relationship atmosphere.

By understanding and appreciating these beneficial features, both partners can develop a relationship that respects the particular strengths and virtues that ADHD can give.

It is very vital to combine support and understanding with the issues that ADHD can potentially offer. By working together as a team and enjoying one other's strengths, the partnership can thrive, and both persons can experience a meaningful and loving connection.

# Chapter 5

## <u>WHEN YOUR BOYFRIEND HAS ADHD</u>

When your boyfriend has ADHD, active listening and efficient communication become even more crucial in maintaining a solid and understanding relationship.

Misunderstandings could emerge due to the difficulties linked with ADHD, such as inattention and impulsivity. To increase communication and prevent misconceptions, use the following tips:

**1. Choose the Right Time and Place:** Find a peaceful and comfortable environment for essential interactions. Minimize distractions, such as loud noises or technological gadgets, to enhance focus during discussions.

**2. Use Eye Contact:** Maintain eye contact whether speaking or listening. This easy approach could make both couples feel more connected and active in the talk.

**3. Practice Patience:** Be patient and let your guy with ADHD to express himself fully. Avoid interrupting, and give him ample time to gather his ideas and present his opinion.

**4. Active Listening Techniques:** Show active listening by nodding, using vocal signs (e.g., "I see," "Go on," "Tell me more"), and paraphrasing what he said to reinforce your expertise.

**5. Use Empathetic Language:** Demonstrate empathy and understanding by utilizing comments such as, "I can see why that's frustrating," or "That sounds challenging, how can I support you?"

**6. Clarify and Confirm:** If you are unclear about something, ask for clarification to prevent misunderstandings. Repeat back what you heard to verify you interpreted it correctly.

**7. Avoid Blame and Criticism:** Focus on the matter at hand rather than blaming or criticizing your partner. Use "I" statements to communicate how you feel instead of pointing fingers.

**8. Be Mindful of Nonverbal Communication:** Pay attention to nonverbal signs, such as body language and tone of voice. Nonverbal cues can convey emotions and offer more significance to the discourse.

**9. Use Visual Aids:** Utilize visual aids, such as charts, calendars, or lists, to help in organizing and planning. Visual tools can make discussions about timetables and responsibilities more approachable and less scary.

**10. Set Clear Expectations:** Communicate honestly about your wants and expectations in the partnership. Establishing a common knowledge of commitments can reduce misunderstandings and potential disputes.

**11. Allow Time for Processing:** Recognize that your guy with ADHD may require extra time to comprehend information or make judgments. Be patient and avoid pressuring him for immediate solutions.

**12. Avoid Overloading with Information:** Break down tough topics or undertakings into smaller, more manageable chunks. This strategy can assist your partner with ADHD absorb information without feeling overwhelmed.

**13. Use Positive Reinforcement:** Praise your partner for efforts made to improve communication and active listening. Positive encouragement could drive him to continue improving his listening abilities.

**14. Seek Couples Therapy:** Consider attending couples therapy together to gain efficient communication strategies and receive help from a therapist with experience in ADHD-related marital challenges.

**15. Encourage Open Communication:** Create a secure climate for open communication where both parties can communicate their feelings and concerns without fear of judgment or condemnation.

**16. Establish Signal Words or Phrases:** Introduce specific signal words or phrases that can help redirect the conversation if either partner feels overwhelmed or distracted. For example, adopting phrases like "pause" or "let's take a breather" can provide a gentle reminder to regroup and refocus.

**17. Be Mindful of Emotional Triggers:** Recognize emotional triggers that could lead to misunderstandings or arguments. Both sides should be conscious of their emotional states throughout discussions and take breaks if needed to avoid growing tensions.

**18. Create Written Summaries:** After key discussions, consider writing down the essential points and conclusions stated. This technique can serve as a reference point to avoid misremembering or misinterpreting agreements.

**19. Utilize Technology:** Leverage technology to enhance communication and organization. Shared calendars, task management apps, and note-taking tools can foster teamwork and prevent misinterpretation.

**20. Plan Check-In Meetings:** Schedule regular check-in meetings to discuss the status of existing tasks, projects, and relationship dynamics. Consistent communication helps avoid challenges from building up and becoming unmanageable.

**21. Encourage Open inquiry:** Instead of presuming understanding, encourage open questions to clarify each other's thoughts and sentiments. For example, asking "How do you feel about this?" or "What are your thoughts on the matter?" can lead to more lengthy discussions.

**22. Take Breaks in Heated Moments:** If conversations grow tense or heated, take a pause and provide each other some room to cool down. Returning to the argument with a calmer manner could lead to more constructive dialogue.

**23. Appreciate Progress:** Acknowledge and appreciate the progress gained in increased communication and active listening. Positive reinforcement can drive both partners to continue working on their communication skills.

**24. Practice Mindfulness:** Incorporate mindfulness practices into your normal routine to stay present and aware during encounters. Techniques such as deep breathing and grounding exercises can help control distractions and boost attention.

**25. Share Responsibility for Communication Improvement:** Recognize that effective communication is a shared undertaking. Both partners should be willing to learn and grow together, actively contributing to better communication and preventing misunderstandings.

**26. Emphasize Positivity:** Focus on the positive aspects of your relationship and your partner's strengths. A helpful and cheery approach can develop a sense of security and trust in the partnership.

**27. Maintain a Sense of Humor:** Humor helps reduce stressful circumstances and brings a light-hearted attitude to unpleasant topics. Finding chances to laugh together can enhance your bond and make speaking more pleasurable.

**28. Cultivate Emotional closeness:** Encourage emotional connection by discussing your views, feelings, and experiences with each other. Being vulnerable with one another can increase your emotional connection and understanding.

**29. Be Flexible in Your Communication Style:** Recognize that excellent communication may necessitate altering your approach depending on the scenario and your partner's requests. Flexibility can lead to more successful conversations.

**30. Show Appreciation:** Express gratitude for your partner's efforts to improve communication and active listening. Feeling respected and appreciated encourages further progress in these areas.

By implementing these recommendations, you can build a helpful and understanding communication culture within your partnership. welcome the learning process together, and welcome challenges as chances for growth and connection.

As you both actively work on enhancing your communication skills, misunderstandings can be removed, and your relationship can grow in an atmosphere of trust, love, and respect.

# **<u>CREATING BOUNDARIES</u>**

Boundaries play a vital role in treating ADHD-related issues and sustaining mutual respect in relationships. When one partner has ADHD, creating and maintaining clear boundaries helps offer a supportive and controlled climate that benefits both partners.

Here's an in-depth lecture on how boundaries can be key in managing ADHD and developing respect:

1. **Establishing Structure and Consistency:** Boundaries create a predictable structure in daily living, which can be particularly useful for someone with ADHD. Consistent routines and expectations help minimize feelings of overload and anxiety, helping your spouse to better manage their time and duties.

**2. Clarifying duties:** Clearly defined boundaries can assist explain each partner's obligations and tasks within the partnership. This clarity minimizes the possibility of misunderstandings and frustration, as each person knows their place and what is expected of them.

**3. Encouraging Open conversation:** Setting limitations includes open and honest conversation between partners. Discussing individual requirements and limitations honestly allows both persons to discuss their difficulties and find solutions collaboratively.

**4. Managing Distractions:** Boundaries can assist limit distractions in the surroundings, which can be particularly advantageous for persons with ADHD. Establishing designated quiet places and removing interruptions during critical work can enhance focus and productivity.

**5. Promoting Emotional Safety:** Boundaries give a safe place where both partners can express their feelings without fear of judgment or condemnation. Emotional safety is crucial for building connection and encouraging honest discourse.

**6. Avoiding Overwhelm:** ADHD can make multitasking and juggling too many obligations overwhelming. Boundaries assist emphasize critical chores and allow your spouse to focus on one item at a time, lowering stress and potential fatigue.

**7. Respecting Time Management:** Set time boundaries to ensure that both spouses have committed time for autonomous pursuits, self-care, and leisure. This balance removes animosity and develops self-regulation.

**8. Managing Impulsivity:** For individuals with ADHD, impulsivity can lead to difficulty in decision-making and impulse control. Establishing restrictions around impulsive acts can help your partner pause and think about their decisions more deliberately.

**9. Encouraging Self-Advocacy:** Boundaries encourage your partner with ADHD to advocate for their needs and communicate when they require help or modifications. This fosters a sense of autonomy and self-awareness.

**10. Enhancing Conflict Resolution:** Clearly defined limits make addressing conflicts more doable. When both couples realize one other's boundaries, they can tackle challenges with empathy and respect.

**11. Teaching and Learning Boundaries:** Boundaries can be a fantastic tool for teaching and reinforcing social skills. Couples can learn together about healthy boundaries and implement them in their relationship, which can have good ramifications outside of the partnership.

**12. Building Trust:** Respecting each other's boundaries creates trust in the partnership. When both partners feel heard and understood, they are more likely to trust one another's intentions and feel secure in the partnership.

**13. Preventing Codependency:** Boundaries assist retain individuality within the partnership, preventing codependent dynamics. Each partner's independence and unique character are protected, leading to a happier and more balanced union.

**14. Encouraging Self-Care:** Boundaries encourage both couples to prioritize self-care. Encouraging your partner with ADHD to take breaks, manage stress, and engage in activities they like is crucial for general well-being.

**15. Minimizing External Stressors:** Establishing boundaries with external influences, such as work-related stress or social commitments, can assist manage external demands that can exacerbate ADHD symptoms.

**16. Enhancing Empathy and Understanding:** Boundaries assist couples to better understand each other's needs and limitations. By respecting limitations, both partners can acquire a deeper sense of empathy, comprehending the impact of ADHD on their partner's daily life.

**17. Preventing Burnout:** For the partner without ADHD, defining boundaries could be crucial for preventing burnout and caregiving tiredness. Taking care of oneself and establishing restrictions on caregiving commitments ensure that both partners have the energy and emotional resources to support each other efficiently.

**18. Supporting Growth and Development:** Boundaries offer a framework for personal growth and development. Each partner can pursue their interests, hobbies, and personal objectives without feeling confined by the relationship.

**19. Balancing Emotional closeness and independence:** Boundaries help achieve a balance between emotional closeness and personal independence. Couples might have intense emotional ties while yet preserving a sense of individuality.

**20. Encouraging Responsible Decision-Making:** Setting boundaries around financial problems and impulsive spending could help your partner with ADHD gain responsible decision-making abilities.

**21. Creating a Partnership of Equals:** Mutual respect for limits fosters an environment where both partners' needs are valued equally. This equality increases the relationship and promotes a sense of teamwork.

**22. Supporting Accommodations and approaches:** Boundaries can help implement accommodations and approaches for treating ADHD. For example, agreeing to use visual aids, organizing tools, or scheduling programs can boost your partner's executive functioning.

**23. Reinforcing Personal Boundaries:** Boundaries can remind individuals with ADHD to respect their personal boundaries, such as recognizing when they need to take breaks, delegate responsibilities, or seek support.

**24. Empowering Self-Expression:** Boundaries encourage open self-expression and sharing of thoughts and emotions.

Feeling heard and valued in the relationship can increase confidence and self-esteem.

**25. Strengthening Emotional Connection:** Setting limits allows partners to be vulnerable with one other. Sharing individual boundaries and respecting them deepens the emotional connection and strengthens the partnership.

**26. Encouraging Flexibility:** Boundaries can promote flexibility and adaptability in the partnership. As the expectations of both parties evolve, the boundaries can be adjusted to suit these changes.

**27. Building a Culture of Respect:** A relationship founded on defined boundaries generates a culture of respect. Both partners learn to value each other's needs and honor their boundaries.

**28. Navigating Social situations:** Discussing and understanding each other's boundaries helps assist navigate social circumstances that may cause ADHD-related concerns. It helps both partners to assist each other in social circumstances.

**29. Addressing Avoidance and Procrastination:** Boundaries can help handle avoidance and procrastination in the relationship. By outlining realistic goals and timetables, both couples may work together to handle tasks effectively.

**30. Improving Relationship Satisfaction:** Overall, creating and respecting boundaries in a relationship when one person has ADHD can lead to increased relationship satisfaction. It creates a safe and supportive basis for tackling the issues and strengths that ADHD brings to the connection.

Defining limits is a shared process that demands open communication, sensitivity, and a willingness to listen to each other's needs. It's vital to approach boundary-setting with compassion, acknowledging that it is about providing a space where both couples can thrive and grow together.

As boundaries are formed and respected, the relationship can become a source of strength and support, allowing both individuals to mature and address ADHD-related challenges with resilience and understanding.

# Chapter 6

## **TREATMENTS**

When your partner has ADHD, several treatment alternatives are accessible to assist regulate the symptoms and boost his general well-being. The most effective treatment strategy typically incorporates a combination of strategies suited to his individual requirements and circumstances. Here are several therapy possibilities for ADHD:

## **MEDICATION**

- <u>Stimulant medications:</u> These are the most usually prescribed drugs for ADHD and function by boosting the levels of particular neurotransmitters in the brain. They can assist in boosting focus, attentiveness, and impulse control.

- <u>Non-Stimulant Medications:</u> In instances where stimulant medications are not appropriate or well-tolerated, non-stimulant medications may be advised. These medicines act differently yet can still help manage ADHD symptoms.

## Behavioral Therapy

- <u>Cognitive Behavioral Therapy (CBT):</u> CBT can offer coping strategies, organizational abilities, and time management techniques to address challenges associated to ADHD.

- <u>Parent Training and Education:</u> If your partner has children, parent training can help him build suitable parenting skills to support children with ADHD.

## Coaching and Skill-Building

- <u>ADHD Coaching:</u> A professional ADHD coach may work with your spouse to develop targets, build organizing skills, and improve time management.

- <u>Executive Function Coaching:</u> This kind of coaching focuses on increasing executive function skills, such as planning, prioritizing, and self-monitoring.

## **Psychoeducation**

- <u>Learning about ADHD:</u> Education on the illness can assist your boyfriend to understand his challenges and strengths better, leading to more effective self-management.

## **Support Groups**

- Joining ADHD support groups or online forums can bring beneficial ideas, encouragement, and a sense of belonging to others suffering similar challenges.

## **Lifestyle Modifications**

- <u>Regular Exercise:</u> Physical activity can help reduce hyperactivity and impulsivity while increasing mood and general well-being.

- <u>Healthy Diet:</u> A balanced diet rich in nutrients can favorably increase brain function and concentration.

- <u>Sufficient Sleep:</u> Ensuring enough restful sleep may greatly enhance attention and minimize ADHD-related symptoms.


## Time Management Strategies

- <u>Using Timers and Alarms:</u> Setting reminders and using timers will assist your spouse keep on track with tasks and appointments.

- <u>Breaking activities into Smaller bits:</u> Dividing activities into manageable pieces might make them less scary and more achievable.

## Environmental Modifications

- <u>Creating a Clutter-Free Environment:</u> An ordered and clutter-free living and working place helps enhance focus and remove distractions.

- <u>Minimizing Distractions:</u> Limiting background noise and interruptions helps increase concentration.

## <u>Stress Reduction Techniques</u>

- <u>Mindfulness & Meditation:</u> Practicing mindfulness can help reduce stress and enhance attention.

- <u>Tension-Relief Activities:</u> Engaging in hobbies or activities that your boyfriend enjoys could provide a good release for tension.

## <u>Collaboration with Healthcare Professionals</u>

- <u>Regular Check-Ins:</u> Encourage your boyfriend to have regular check-ins with his healthcare practitioner to monitor his progress and change treatment as appropriate.

- <u>Collaborative Decision-Making:</u> Involve your partner in the treatment decision-making process to ensure a sense of ownership and commitment to the chosen therapies.

## Time Awareness Strategies

- <u>Use Visual Timers:</u> Visual timers, such as hourglasses or countdown clocks, can help your person better manage time and move between activities.

- <u>Set Alarms for Transitions:</u> Alarms can warn him when it's time to transfer jobs or prepare for impending occasions, minimizing potential distractions.

## Assistive Technology

- <u>Utilize Productivity Apps:</u> There are various apps intended to benefit persons with ADHD with organization, task management, and time tracking.

- <u>Electronic Reminders:</u> Digital calendars and reminder apps can help your partner remain on top of appointments and obligations.

## **Acceptance and Self-Compassion**
- <u>Encourage Self-Awareness:</u> Help your boyfriend realize his ADHD-related strengths and issues without judgment.

- <u>Promote Self-Compassion:</u> Encourage him to be kind to himself and understand that treating ADHD can be a journey with ups and downs.

## **Relationship Communication Strategies**
- <u>Open and Honest Dialogue:</u> Encourage open communication regarding how ADHD

effects your boyfriend and the relationship dynamics.

- <u>Active Listening:</u> Both partners should actively listen and validate each other's feelings and opinions.

## Relationship Counseling

- Consider attending relationship counseling jointly to address any challenges that ADHD may pose to the partnership. A trained therapist can provide tools and strategies for keeping a healthy and supportive relationship.

## Career and Workplace Support

- Adjustments at Work: If your boyfriend suffers trouble in his career owing to ADHD symptoms, he may consider requesting for workplace adjustments or speaking with human services about supporting measures.

## <u>Self-Advocacy Skills</u>

- Empower your boyfriend to advocate for his needs in numerous instances, whether at work, in social situations, or hospital settings.

## <u>Encourage Self-Regulation Techniques</u>

- <u>Breathing Exercises:</u> Teach relaxation techniques and deep breathing exercises to assist him manage stress and regulate emotions.
- <u>Mindfulness exercises:</u> Engaging in mindfulness activities can boost focus and reduce impulsivity.

## <u>Celebrate Progress and Success</u>

- Acknowledge your boyfriend's efforts in managing ADHD and enjoy his achievements, no matter how minor they may seem.

### Flexibility and Adaptability

- Recognize that treating ADHD can involve trial and error. Be flexible in altering tactics as needed to determine what works best for him.

### Empowerment and Independence

- Encourage your boyfriend to take an active role in his treatment and self-management. Empowering him to make decisions regarding his care builds a sense of freedom.

### Emphasize the Positives

- Focus on the strengths and positive traits that ADHD can give to the relationship and other spheres of life.

Being a supporting partner and working together to adopt effective techniques can give a strong base for a loving and fulfilling relationship, where both partners thrive and grow together.

Additionally, becoming aware of ADHD and its impact can enable you to be an educated and empathetic ally in supporting your boyfriend's well-being.

# Chapter 7

## <u>SELF-CARE</u>

When your boyfriend has ADHD, it's vital to take care of yourself to maintain your well-being and navigate the special challenges that may occur in the relationship.

Practicing self-help activities can allow you to establish understanding, patience, and resilience while nurturing a healthy and supportive partnership. Here are numerous self-help ideas for yourself when your boyfriend has ADHD:

**1. Educate Yourself about ADHD:** Knowledge is vital to understanding the impact of ADHD on your boyfriend and your relationship. Read trustworthy publications, attend courses, or join support groups to get essential insights.

**2. Practice Patience and Empathy:** ADHD-related symptoms could be tough at times, but practicing patience and empathy can help you respond with understanding and compassion.

**3. Set Boundaries:** Establish clear boundaries to safeguard your well-being and explain your requirements successfully. Boundaries can assist manage tension and establish a nice balance in the partnership.

**4. Communicate Openly:** Foster open discussion with your sweetheart about how ADHD influences both of you. Be honest about your thoughts and anxieties, and encourage him to do the same.

**5. Seek Emotional Support:** Share your experiences with close friends, family members, or a support group. Talking about your feelings could give you relief and validation.

**6. Prioritize Self-Care:** Take care of your physical and emotional needs. Engage in things that offer you delight, practice relaxing techniques, and create time for pastimes you enjoy.

**7. Set Realistic Expectations:** Understand that ADHD may impair your partner's ability to accomplish particular tasks or follow through on commitments. Set moderate expectations and applaud progress, no matter how modest.

**8. Explore Coping methods Together:** Work constructively with your partner to explore coping techniques that benefit both of you. Encourage him to use tools that improve organization and time management.

**9. Focus on the Positive:** Recognize and appreciate the special assets and features your boyfriend provides to the relationship, outside the constraints of ADHD.

**10. Maintain Individuality:** Nurture your hobbies, objectives, and friendships. Having a life outside of the partnership is vital for personal growth and satisfaction.

**11. Seek Professional Support:** If needed, try obtaining help from a therapist or counselor who specializes in ADHD-related relationship concerns.

**12. Practice Mindfulness:** Cultivate mindfulness skills to stay present and nonjudgmental amid difficult conditions. Mindfulness can reduce stress and enhance emotional resilience.

**13. Practice Active Listening:** Be attentive and interested when your sweetheart communicates. Practice active listening to display empathy and understanding.

**14. Appreciate Your Progress:** Acknowledge your efforts in adapting to the barriers of the relationship and appreciate the progress and insights you get along the path.

**15. Encourage Self-Advocacy:** Empower your partner with ADHD to advocate for his needs and speak honestly. Encouraging self-advocacy improves mutual understanding and collaboration.

**16. Develop Coping Techniques for Yourself:** Identify coping ways that assist you handle stress and emotional concerns when dealing with ADHD-related conditions.

**17. Set Aside Time for Yourself:** Carve out alone time to replenish and ponder. Having personal space allows you to decompress and maintain emotional balance.

**18. Avoid Taking Things Personally:** Remember that ADHD symptoms are not a reflection of your worth as a partner. Avoid taking behavior personally and focus on healthy communication.

**19. Learn to De-escalate Tensions:** Develop techniques to de-escalate contentious conditions, such as taking a break when emotions run high, and returning to the dispute when both sides are calmer.

**20. Stay Flexible:** Be flexible in your expectations and adjust to the ever-changing nature of ADHD. Flexibility provides a more adaptive and resilient collaboration.

**21. Recognize Your Emotional Limits:** Identify your emotional limits and transmit them effectively to your partner. Let him know how particular actions or behaviors affect you emotionally, generating greater understanding and respect.

**22. Seek Support from Others:** Connect with friends, relatives, or support groups that understand and empathize with the issues of being in a relationship with someone with ADHD. Sharing experiences with others can generate affirmation and helpful ideas.

**23. Tackle Co-Occurring barriers:** If you have other barriers in addition to ADHD in your relationship, such as communication challenges or intimacy concerns, obtain guidance from professionals to tackle these elements constructively.

**24. Celebrate minor accomplishments:** Celebrate the tiny successes and positive moments in your relationship. Focusing on the good can increase your emotional connection and generate a sense of gratitude.

**25. Develop a Sense of Humor:** Maintaining a sense of humor can assist reduce stressful circumstances and offer lightness to challenging moments. Finding opportunities to laugh together helps develop a healthy atmosphere.

**26. Practice Compassionate Communication:** Use compassionate and non-blaming language when discussing challenges related with ADHD. Avoid casting blame and instead focus on finding answers together.

**27. Engage in Joint Problem-Solving:** Work cooperatively to discover creative solutions to difficulties that arise due to ADHD. Brainstorm ideas together and aid each other in adopting successful solutions.

**28. Take Breaks When Needed:** If you or your partner feel overwhelmed or pushed, take breaks from hard conversations. Time away might provide chance for introspection and prevent future escalation.

**29. Be Mindful of any stresses:** Be mindful of any stresses that may undermine your relationship, such as work responsibilities or financial troubles. Managing external stress can relieve strain inside the partnership.

**30. Appreciate Each Other's Growth:** Acknowledge and appreciate each other's growth and efforts in managing ADHD-related challenges. A kind and encouraging attitude can reinforce favorable changes.

**31. Maintain Your Identity:** Nurture your identity and hobbies outside the partnership. Having your activities and passions enriches your life and contributes favorably to the partnership.

**32. Acknowledge Your Feelings:** Validate your feelings and emotions, even when they may appear harsh or conflicting. Self-awareness permits you to address your emotions successfully.

**33. Create Realistic Expectations for Yourself:** Avoid perfectionism and create realistic expectations for your place in the partnership. Embrace the mistakes and focus on progress rather than unattainable ambitions.

**34. Practice Gratitude:** Cultivate a habit of expressing gratitude for your partner and your relationship. Gratitude can increase your link and generate a pleasant attitude toward the partnership.

**35. Nurture Emotional Intimacy:** Continue to establish emotional intimacy with your companion. Emotional connection can give a foundation of support amid adverse conditions.

**36. Focus on Shared Interests:** Engage in activities or hobbies you both like, creating opportunity for quality time and shared experiences.

**37. Prioritize Your Well-Being:** Make self-care a priority in your life. Take time for things that replenish and energize you.

**38. Avoid Blaming ADHD for Everything:** Recognize that not all interpersonal issues are primarily connected to ADHD. Avoid attributing every issue to the disease, as other causes may be at play.

**39. Encourage Self-Reflection:** Encourage your partner to engage in self-reflection and personal improvement. Support his eagerness to learn more about himself and improve self-awareness.

**40. Celebrate Love and Connection:** Appreciate the love and connection you share with your partner, focusing on the special link you've built despite the trials.

Practicing self-help in a relationship with ADHD is a continuous journey of growth and learning. Be patient with yourself and your spouse as you negotiate the ups and downs together. Embrace the process, appreciate the development, and embrace the love and understanding that you create inside the partnership.

www.ingramcontent.com/pod-product-compliance
Lightning Source LLC
Chambersburg PA
CBHW071609270726
48661CB00019B/1937